THE LIFE OF BUDDHA

[FROM PRINCE SIDDHARTHA TO BUDDHA]

TEXT: GEORGE HULSKRAMER
ILLUSTRATIONS: BIJAY RAJ SHAKYA AND RAJU BABU SHAKYA
PUBLISHED BY BINKEY KOK - DIEVER/HOLLAND

DATA ROYAL LIBRARY, THE HAGUE, THE NETHERLANDS

Hulskramer, George

The life of Buddha : from prince Siddhartha to Buddha /
George Hulskramer ; [ill.: Bijay Raj Shakya ... et al.].
– Diever : Binkey Kok. – Ill.
ISBN 90-74597-17-3
Subject headings ; Buddhism-comic

Colofon

Publisher	:	Binkey Kok, Diever, Holland
		tel. 05219-1603, fax: 05219-1925
Cover Design	:	Jaap Koning BNO, Amsterdam
Scenario	:	George Hulskramer, Amsterdam
Drawings and coloring	:	Byaj Raj Shakya en Raju Babu Shakya. Kathmandu
Caracters	:	Frits Jonker, Amsterdam
Nepal Editor	:	Tula N, Shakya Kathmandu
Production	:	Jaap Verheij, Fluitenberg
Printed by	:	Bariet, Ruinen
Bound by	:	Abbringh, Groningen

Distributed in the U.S.A. by
Samuel Welser Inc. Box 612, York Beach
Maine 03910

© 1995 by Binkey Kok

TWO THOUSAND FIVE HUNDRED YEARS AGO. DUSK IS FALLING IN THE LAND OF THE SHAKYA'S, THE PRESENT SOUTH NEPAL KING SHUDODANA AND HIS WIFE MAYA ARE REFLECTING ON A WELL-SPENT DAY.

LET'S GO TO BED EARLY TONIGHT. YOU LOOK TIRED, DEAREST.

TWENTY-FIVE YEARS OF WAR. I HOPE THE COUNTRY WILL FARE BETTER IN THE NEXT TWENTY-FIVE YEARS.

COME, LET'S GO.

THEY WALK BACK TO THE PALACE.

3

LOOK, DARLING, PERHAPS THE STARS WILL BRING US LUCK.

DUSK IS FALLING.

IT'S A LONG TIME SINCE WE WERE IN THE GARDEN TOGETHER.

THEY ENTER THE ROYAL BEDCHAMBER.

THE KING WISHES TO CLOSE THE ROOF.

I'D RATHER WISH YOU LEFT IT OPEN, DARLING.

BE PATIENT. I'M COMING.

MAYA REMOVES HER JEWELLERY.

6

NINE MONTHS LATER, MAYA BIDS FAREWELL TO GIVE BIRTH IN THE HOUSE WHERE SHE WAS BORN.

SHE DRIVES OFF WITH HER SISTER PRADJAPATHI.

ON THE WAY, MAYA FEELS THE FIRST LABOUR PAINS.

OH, PRADJAPATHI, WE MUST STOP, I CAN'T GO ON! I MUST REST.

THEY STOP AT THE EDGE OF A WOOD.

TAKE ME TO A PLACE WHERE I CAN GIVE BIRTH.

SOME SERVANTS PREPARE A BED OF LEAVES FOR THE QUEEN.

MAYA LISTENS TO THE BIRDS.

7

THE KING AND QUEEN SHOW THEIR SON TO THE GUESTS.

THERE IS AN ENDLESS LINE OF VISITORS.

ASITA?

AN ANCIENT HERMIT DRESSED IN RAGS APPEARS...

ASITA, THE GREAT SEER! WHAT AN HONOUR, WELCOME.

SIT DOWN ON MY THRONE, ASITA.

HERE, ASITA, MY SON, PREDICT HIS FUTURE.

THE GODS HAVE WHISPERED TO ME THAT YOUR SON WILL BE A RELIGIOUS WORLD TEACHER.

THE SEER CONCENTRATES, THE GUEST WAIT EXPECTANTLY.

PEOPLE, THIS IS THE NEW WORLD TEACHER.

HE POINTS OUT THE SIGN OF THE WHEEL ON THE SOLES OF HIS FEED, THE SIGNS ON HIS FINGERS, HIS THIN CROWN, HIS LONG EARLOBES.

THE QUEEN PULLS THE CHILD FROM ASITA'S HANDS.

DO BE CAREFUL.

?!

?!

DON'T BE AFRAID, YOUR MAJESTY. THERE IS NOTHING THE MATTER WITH YOUR SON.

WHY DO YOU SUDDENLY LOOK SO SAD?

I DO NOT NEED A WORLD TEACHER AT ALL. A SUCCESSOR TO MY THRONE IS WHAT I NEED.

UNFORTUNATELY THE SIGNS DO NOT INDICATE THIS.

NEVERTHELESS, MY SON SHALL SUCCEED ME AND BECOME KING. MY WILL IS LAW.

JUST WAIT, MY KING, NO MAN CAN DEFY THE WILL OF THE GODS.

I AM THE KING AND MY WILL SHALL BE DONE.

THE KING WALKS OUT IN A RAGE, LEAVING THE OTHERS BEHIND IN CONSTERNATION.

OF COURSE MY SON WILL BE KING ONE DAY, WHO ELSE COULD SUCCEED ME?

I DON'T KNOW,

LATER IN BED. THE KING SAYS: "OH, WHAT AM I WORRYING ABOUT? SEERS CAN MAKE MISTAKES TOO,"

THE GODS DETERMINE THE FATE OF MAN, EVEN A KING CANNOT CHANGE THAT,

I THINK HE IS ASLEEP,

ZZZZZZ

MAYA REMEMBERS THE VOICE SHE HEARD A FEW DAYS AGO,

YOUR SON WILL BE A WORLD TEACHER. BUT, YOU WILL NOT LIVE TO SEE IT, YOUR TASK IN THIS LIFE ON EARTH IS ALMOST COMPLETE,

SHALL I TELL HIM? NO, HE HAS ENOUGH PROBLEMS,

12

ONE DAY AFTER THE FUNERAL...

CALL THE MINISTERS TOGETHER AS QUICKLY AS POSSIBLE. UNDER NO CIRCUMSTANCES MAY MY SON EXCHANGE THE WORLDLY LIFE FOR A RELIGIOUS LIFE. WE MUST DO EVERYTHING POSSIBLE TO ENSURE THAT HE SUCCEEDS ME TO THE THRONE.

THE OLDEST MINISTER SPEAKS...

YOU NEED NOT BE AFRAID, ONLY POOR PEOPLE TURN TO THE GODS. YOUR SON IS...

I DO NOT WANT TO TAKE ANY RISKS, MAKE SURE THAT THE YOUNG PRINCE DOES NOT LACK FOR ANYTHING.

THE YOUNG SIDDHARTHA TAKES HIS FIRST STEPS IN THE WALLED GARDEN.

THE LITTLE PRINCE IS VERY SELF-CONTAINED. WATCHED BY PRADJAPATHI AND HIS FATHER HE LIKES TO PLAY WITH ANIMALS BEST OF ALL.

15

He wraps the wounded swan in his shirt.

Someone runs into the garden.

?!

He recognizes his cousin, Devadatta.

Siddhartha, I've shot a swan!

Then he sees the swan.

Give it to me, Siddhartha! I was the one who shot it down!

No, you can't have it!

This creature needs looking after.

They each pull at the swan for a long time.

Let us put the case to the Brahmans.

Alright, we will.

Together they walk to the palace.

17

SUDDENLY EVERYONE IS SILENT.

SIDDHARTHA IS RIGHT, ALL LIFE COMES FROM GOD. ANYONE WHO HELPS TO PRESERVE LIFE ACTS MORE IN ACCORDANCE WITH GOD'S WILL THAN A PERSON WHO DESTROYS LIFE. THERE- FORE SIDDHARTHA DESERVES OUR SYMPATHY.

ASITA IS RIGHT, WE GRANT THE CREATURE TO SIDDHARTHA.

I CAN'T TELL YOU HOW GRATEFUL I AM.

ONE FINE DAY, THE PRINCE, NOW AGED TWENTY, IS SEATED AMONGST THE ANIMALS IN THE PALACE GARDEN.

?!

IF ONLY, HE DOESN'T... I MUST DO SOMETHING, BEFORE HE...

YOUR SON IS MUCH TOO RESERVED, HOW WILL HE BE ABLE TO GOVERN THE COUNTRY WHEN THE TIME COMES?

THERE IS ANOTHER PROBLEM: HE IS BECOMING IN- CREASINGLY IN- QUISITIVE ABOUT THE WORLD.

WHAT IS THERE, BEYOND THE WALLS?

IS THIS ALL...?

WHY ARE WE ALIVE?

WHY DO WE...

WHAT IS LIFE?

I WOULD LIKE...

I HAVE ALWAYS TOLD HIM THAT EVERYTHING IS THE SAME THERE AS IT IS HERE.

I GET THE FEELING HE DOES NOT BELIEVE ME, WHAT SHOULD I DO?

18

THE PRINCE IS WASHED AND BATHED.

HIS SERVANTS DRESS HIM FOR THE DRIVE.

THE KING GIVES THE CHARIOTEER THE FINAL INSTRUCTIONS.

ONE LAST THING.

ONLY TALK OF SUPERFICIAL MATTERS, CHANNA.

WHEN THEY HAVE DEPARTED...

I ONLY HOPE THIS DRIVER DOES NOT GIVE MY SON ANY DOUBTS ABOUT HIS VOCATION AS A RULER.

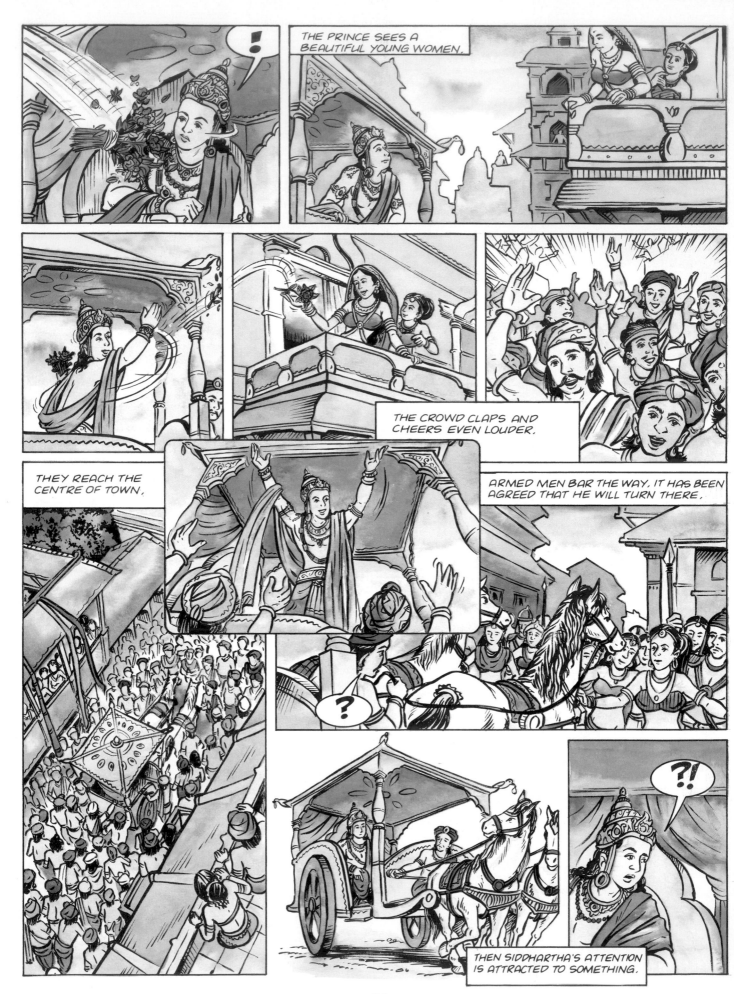

THE PRINCE SEES A BEAUTIFUL YOUNG WOMEN.

THE CROWD CLAPS AND CHEERS EVEN LOUDER.

THEY REACH THE CENTRE OF TOWN.

ARMED MEN BAR THE WAY, IT HAS BEEN AGREED THAT HE WILL TURN THERE.

THEN SIDDHARTHA'S ATTENTION IS ATTRACTED TO SOMETHING.

HE CANNOT RESTRAIN HIS CURIOSITY.

?!

YOUR HIGH-NESS, STAY HERE!

?!

?!

THEN SIDDHARTHA STANDS STILL...

WHAT ARE THOSE MEN DOING?

COME WITH ME, YOUR HIGNESS, THERE IS NOTHING FOR YOU YOU HERE.

NO!

WHY ARE THOSE PEOPLE HALF NAKED? WHY ARE THEY SO THIN?

OH! GOD!

WHEN THE PRINCE GOES UP TO THEM HE IS EVEN MORE SHOCKED!

?!

YOUR HIGHNESS, LISTEN TO ME! NOT EVERYONE IS AS RICH AS YOU.

THERE ARE PEOPLE WHO HAVE NOTHING TO EAT.

?

WHY DID NO ONE TELL ME ABOUT THIS?

HE LETS CHANNA DRAG HIM BACK TO THE CARRIAGE.

HOW AWFUL!

HE SEES TWO SOLDIERS BEATING UP THE BEGGARS.

CHANNA, WAIT!

THEY ARE DRAGGING THOSE PEOPLE AWAY LIKE ANIMALS... WHY?

I DON'T WANT TO TALK ABOUT THESE THINGS.

I WANT AN ANSWER TO MY QUESTION, CHANNA!

!

I'M SORRY, YOUR HIGHNESS, BUT I CAN'T TALK ABOUT IT.

THE PRINCE INSISTS ON AN ANSWER.

ONCE THOSE TWO BEGGARS LOOKED JUST LIKE THE OTHER PEOPLE BY THE ROADSIDE,

ONCE THEY ALSO SUCKLED AT THEIR MOTHER'S BREAST,

?!

THE PRINCE STANDS UP...

HOW CAN THOSE PEOPLE BECOME SO DECREPIT?

OLD AGE, YOUR HIGHNESS,

I DON'T THINK I SHOULD HAVE SAID THAT,

OLD AGE?

PLEASE SIT DOWN YOUR HIGHNESS.

SIDDHARTHA EXPLODES...

TELL ME CHANNA, WHAT IS OLD AGE?!

TIME RENDERS EVERYTHING OLD AND UGLY, YOUR HIGNESS, IN THE END IT CAUSES EVERYTHING TO WITHER AND SHRIVEL UP,

THE PRINCE SITS DOWN AGAIN, SUNK IN THOUGHT.

HE JUMPS OUT OF THE CARRIAGE ONCE AGAIN,

YOUR HIGHNESS!

!

25

HE DISAPPEARS INTO THE CROWD...

YOUR HIGHNESS, COME BACK!

CHANNA RUNS AFTER HIM...

SIDDHARTHA STANDS STILL IN A MARKET SQUARE,

?!

CHANNA, LET ME GO! WHO IS THAT MAN?

COME WITH ME,

DO ALL PEOPLE LOOK LIKE THIS AT THE END OF THEIR LIFE?

YES, YOUR HIGHNESS. NOW, LET'S GO.

THEY LEAVE THE MARKET SQUARE.

THE PEOPLE START CROWDING AROUND.

THEY WALK AWAY FROM THE CROWD.

LET'S GET OUT OF HERE, YOUR HIGHNESS.

THEY ARE ON THEIR OWN.

THEY HIDE IN AN ALLEYWAY.

I GET THE FEELING THAT YOU'RE HIDING THINGS FROM ME IN THE PALACE. I WANT TO LOOK AROUND A BIT MORE.

PLEASE DON'T GET ME INTO ANY MORE TROUBLE. LET'S GO BACK TO THE CARRIAGE.

27

I CERTAINLY WON'T. GIVE ME YOUR CLOTHES.

AND I WILL GIVE YOU MINE.

ALAS, I MUST OBEY.

THEY EXCHANGE CLOTHES...

SIDDHARTHA HIDES HIS HAIR, AND BLACKENS HIS FACE WITH MUD.

THEY LEAVE THEIR HIDING PLACE.

THEY WALK BACK TO THE SQUARE.

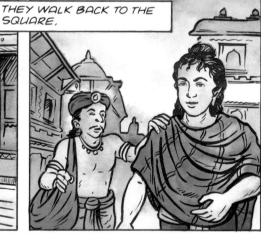

TWO MAN ARE PUSHING A HEAVILY LADEN WAGON.

?

CHANNA EXPLAINS HOW BREAD IS BAKED.

THEY WALK PAST A BUTCHER'S SHOP...

...AND A VEGETABLE STALL. CHANNA EXPLAINS.

AAAAH! THE PAIN!

?

WHERE ARE YOU GOING? WAIT!

THE PRINCE RUNS TOWARDS THE NOISE.

AAAAH!

HE STOPS BY A DILAPIDATED HUT...

?!

HE SEES AN EMACIATED WOMAN.

CHANNA, WHAT IS THE MATTER WITH HER?

SHE LOOKS SERIOUSLY ILL.

ILL?

THE PRINCE LOOKS IN AGAIN.

?!

HE SEES MORE SICK PEOPLE.

ARE THESE PEOPLE ILL TOO?

YES, THERE IS NO HOPE FOR THEM.

THEY CERTAINLY LOOK INCURABLY ILL.

MORE THAN ONE HOUR LATER...

COME ALONG, YOUR HIGHNESS. THERE IS NOTHING FOR US HERE.

WILL I GROW OLD AND SICK TOO?

CHANNA IS IN DOUBT ABOUT THE ANSWER HE SHOULD GIVE.

WELL?

JUST OUTSIDE THE VILLAGE...

WHY CAN'T I LOOK BACK?

ANSWER ME! YOU HEARD WHAT I ASKED, DIDN'T YOU? DO I HAVE TO DISMISS YOU?

?

ALAS, I'VE SAID FAR TOO MUCH ALREADY. I HOPE YOU WON'T TALK TO ANYONE ABOUT THIS.

I PROMISE I WON'T TELL ANYONE.

EVERYONE GROWS OLD, EVEN KINGS AND PRINCES.

?

WHAT DO YOU MEAN? PLEASE SAY THAT AGAIN.

CHANNA REPEATS WHAT HE SAID.

WHY HAS NO ONE EVER TOLD ME ABOUT THIS?

NO ONE DIES WITHOUT BEING SICK AT LEAST ONCE.

DIES?

EXPLAIN YOURSELF, CHANNA.

!

GOOD HEAVENS, NOW WHAT HAVE I SAID?

ALRIGHT, YOUR HIGHNESS, I WILL TELL YOU EVERYTHING.

THE TWO MEN TALK FOR A LONG TIME.

SO EVEN A KING DIES AND CHANGES INTO A CORPSE?

I'M AFRAID THAT IT HAPPENS TO EVERYONE.

?

COULD YOU SHOW ME A CORPSE?

LET'S GO BACK TO THE PALACE. I'LL BE HELD RESPONSIBLE FOR THIS.

IF YOU DO WHAT I ASK, I'LL MAKE SURE THAT NOTHING HAPPENS TO YOU.

BELIEVE ME, CHANNA, THIS IS REALLY VERY IMPORTANT TO ME.

31

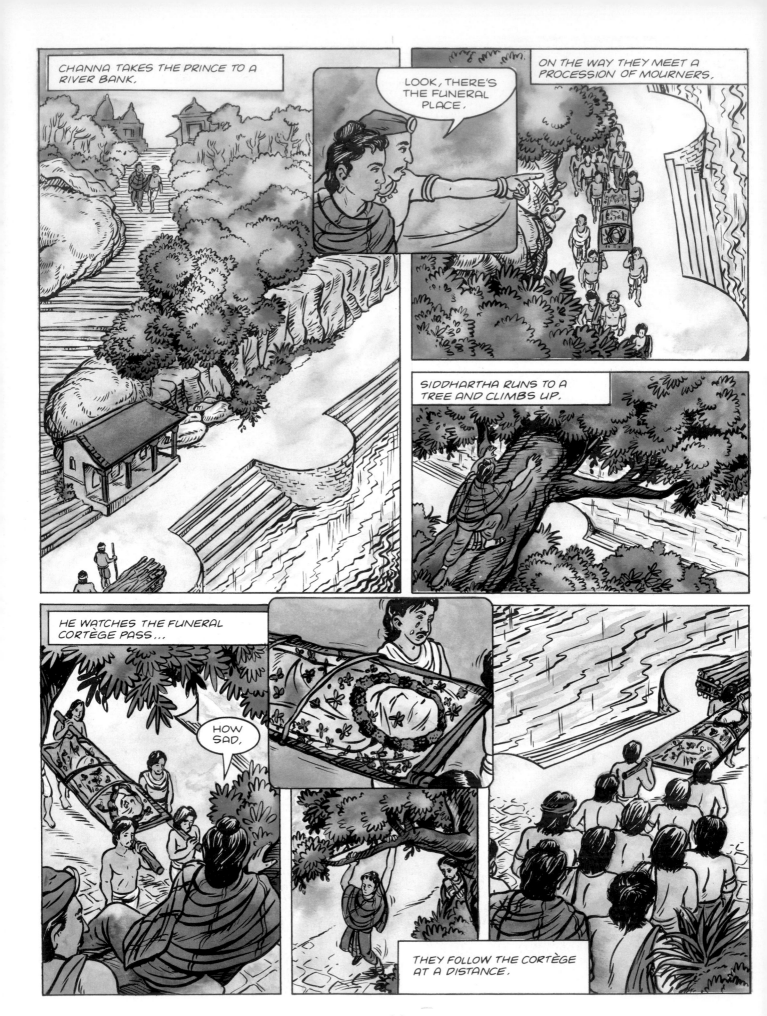

THE CORPSE IS PLACED ON A FUNERAL PYRE...

...ON THE RIVER BANK...

A DEAD MAN...

GOD HAVE PITY!

SIDDHARTHA BENDS OVER THE CORPSE.

COME ON, MAN, MOVE BACK.

GOD HAVE PITY!

HE IS COMPLETELY ENGROSSED IN THE SCENE.

DO YOU UNDERSTAND? THIS IS THE END FOR ALL OF US.

THEY WATCH THE CORPSE BURN.

THE ASHES ARE SCATTERED OVER THE RIVER.

WHEN IT IS ALL OVER...

I THINK WE SHOULD GO BACK NOW, CHANNA.

THE NEXT DAY THE KING IMMEDIATELY CALLS HIS MINISTERS TO HIM.

MY LORDS, WHAT I HAVE ALWAYS FEARED HAS HAPPENED.

MY SON TALKS ONLY ABOUT DEATH, HE HAS NOT LEFT HIS ROOM FOR TWO WHOLE DAYS, AND HE IS VERY ANGRY WITH ME.

CAN I SPEAK?

WHAT DOES HE THINK YOU DID WRONG, SIRE?

I HAVE ALWAYS KEPT QUIET ABOUT THE EXISTENCE OF THINGS LIKE POVERTY, OLD AGE AND DEATH,

I KEPT QUIET ABOUT THESE THINGS TO PROTECT THE BOY FROM HIMSELF, BUT ALAS...

DOES ANYONE HAVE ANY GOOD ADVICE?

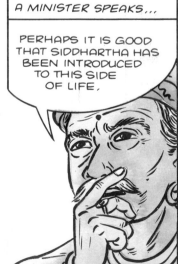

A MINISTER SPEAKS...

PERHAPS IT IS GOOD THAT SIDDHARTHA HAS BEEN INTRODUCED TO THIS SIDE OF LIFE,

34

THEY ALL AIR THEIR VIEWS.

THIS IS ALL VERY WELL, MY DEAR COLLEGUE, BUT SURELY YOU KNOW WHAT ASITA PREDICTED.

WE MUST SAVE MY SON FOR THE THRONE. DOES ANYONE HAVE ANY GOOD IDEAS?

SURELY THERE MUST BE A WAY OF CONVINCING MY SON THAT LIFE IN THIS WORLD HAS PLEASURABLE ASPECTS.

THE KING TURNS TO HIS OLDEST MINISTER.

GANESH, HAVEN'T YOU GOT ANY GOOD IDEAS?

YOUR SON IS A DEEPLY RELIGIOUS MAN WHO ALREADY UNDERSTANDS THE RELATIVE NATURE OF EVERYTHING.

PERHAPS I SHOULD SIMPLY CLOSE THE MEETING.

I HAVE NOT FINISHED YET, YOUR HIGHNESS.

AFTER A LONG SILENCE...

WHY DID YOU NEVER OPT FOR A RELIGIOUS LIFE, YOUR MAJESTY?

SURELY YOU MUST HAVE ASKED YOURSELF WHAT IT IS ALL FOR!

THE KINGS THINKS ABOUT THIS...

WHAT A QUESTION! I WAS RESPONSIBLE FOR MY WIFE AND CHILD.

COULD YOU REPEAT THAT, PLEASE?

THE KING REPEATS HIS WORDS...

THANK YOU, YOUR MAJESTY, THIS IS EXACTLY WHAT I MEANT.

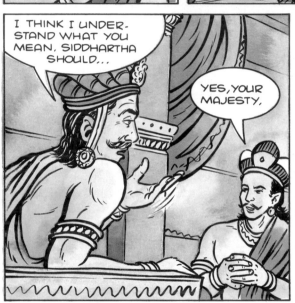

I THINK I UNDERSTAND WHAT YOU MEAN, SIDDHARTHA SHOULD...

YES, YOUR MAJESTY.

EVERYONE LISTENS ATTENTIVELY.

CERTAINLY, YOUR MAJESTY, THE PRINCE NEEDS A WIFE. WHAT MAN IS UNMOVED BY THE MOST BEAUTIFUL OF GOD'S CREATIONS?

THE SOONER WE APPEASE SIDDHARTHA'S RESTLESS SPIRIT, THE BETTER.

EXCUSE MY IMPATIENCE, GANESH, THAT'S CERTAINLY A BRILLIANT IDEA.

THE KING THANKS GANESH.

DEAR MINISTERS, IT'S TRUE THAT MY SON IS STILL A DREAMER, THAT'S PROBABLY BECAUSE HE HAS NO RESPONSIBILITIES AT ALL, WE'RE GOING TO CHANGE THAT AS SOON AS POSSIBLE.

37

HE TAKES A PLACE BEHIND A TABLE LADEN WITH ORNAMENTS. THE KING AND HIS MINISTERS LINE UP ON THE LEFT AND RIGHT.

THE GIRLS WAIT IN A LONG LINE IN FRONT OF THE STAGE,

ONE BY ONE, THEY STEP UP TO THE DAIS.

EACH GIRL RECEIVES A GIFT.

SIDDHARTHA DOES NOT SEEM INTERESTED,

YOUR MAJESTY, IT LOOKS AS TOUGH YOUR SON IS NOT INTERESTED IN WOMEN,

THE PILE OF GIFTS GETS SMALLER...

FINALLY THERE IS ONLY ONE GIRL LEFT, JASODHARA.

WHO ARE YOU?

A FEW WEEKS LATER THE RULERS EMBRACE.

THE TWO KINGS TALK FOR A LONG TIME IN THE PALACE GARDEN.

I GET THE FEELING THAT HE WILL NOT SIMPLY GIVE HIS DAUGHTER TO MY SON.

THERE ARE SO MANY PRINCES WHO WOULD LOVE TO MARRY MY DAUGHTER.

WHAT HAS HE HEARD ABOUT MY SON..?

I SAY THIS BECAUSE MANY STORIES ARE TOLD IN MY COUNTRY ABOUT SIDDHARTHA'S UNWORLD-LINESS.

LET US GATHER TOGETHER ALL THE SUITORS SO THAT THEY CAN COMPETE AGAINST EACH OTHER.

A GOOD IDEA.

THE TWO KINGS SHAKE HANDS ON THE DEAL.

WE WILL AWAIT THE COMPETITION.

FIVE WEEKS LATER THE GREAT DAY ARRIVES, THE MANY GUESTS WAIT, FULL OF EXCITEMENT.

MY SON IS NOT A GREAT ONE FOR COMPETITIVE GAMES, GANESH, I FEAR...

THE KING IS NOT VERY CONFIDENT ABOUT THE OUTCOME...

THE KING SIGNALS TO HIS SON TO COME TO THE ROYAL STAND.

I BEG YOU, SIDDHARTHA, WITHDRAW. IT'S STILL POSSIBLE.

ANYONE WITH STRENGTH OF SPIRIT ALSO HAS PHYSICAL STRENGTH, FATHER.

THE FIRST SECTION IS ARCHERY.

THOK

POOR SIDDHARTHA, HE WILL REALLY LOSE FACE.

DEVADATTA, THE PRINCE'S COUSIN, SHOOTS STRAIGHT INTO THE BULL'S EYE.

FINALLY IT IS SIDDHARTHA'S TURN...

43

44

A FEW YEARS LATER...

I CANNOT FIND WORDS TO EXPRESS MY HAPPINESS.

I NEVER THOUGHT YOU WOULD BE A FATHER ONE DAY.

SIDDHARTHA REMAINS SILENT.

WHY IS SIDDHARTHA WALKING AWAY ALL OF A SUDDEN? ISN'T HE HAPPY WITH HIS CHILD?

YOUR SON IS THE MOST INSCRUTABLE PERSON I'VE EVER MET, FATHER.

YOUR SON WAS BOTH HAPPY AND SAD WHEN OUR CHILD WAS BORN. HE IS SAD BECAUSE THE CHILD WILL GROW OLD AND DIE ONE DAY.

MY HUSBAND THINKS VERY DEEPLY ABOUT EVERYTHING. HE WONDERS ABOUT THINGS WHICH WOULD NEVER OCCUR TO ME.

FOR EXAMPLE, WHETHER LOVE IS THE GREATEST GOOD IN LIFE. AFTER ALL, SOONER OR LATER, LOVERS ARE PARTED BY DEATH.

FATHER!

OH, GOD...

OH!

WHEN THE KING HEARS THIS, HE FAINTS AWAY.

47

48

AT HIS WIT'S END, THE KING CALLS FOR GANESH,

YOUR IDEA FOR MY SON'S MARRIAGE WAS BRILLIANT, HAVE YOU ANY MORE SUGGESTIONS?

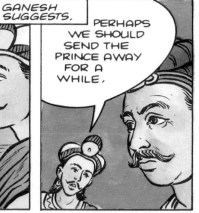
GANESH SUGGESTS,

PERHAPS WE SHOULD SEND THE PRINCE AWAY FOR A WHILE,

GANESH, YOU ARE NOT THINKING STRAIGHT, YOU KNOW WHAT ASITA PREDICTED,

THEY WALK INTO THE GARDEN...

?!

SIDDHARTHA IS LYING ON A BENCH LOOKING BORED,

TELL ME, DO YOU THINK THAT BOY IS HAPPY,

HE DOESN'T LOOK HAPPY,

NOTHING INTERESTS HIM, HE KEEPS TALKING ABOUT WHAT HE SAW IN THE TOWN WHEN HE WENT THERE,

ALAS, FROM THAT TIME EVERYTHING WENT WRONG WITH MY SON,

IT IS IMPOSSIBLE FOR US TO HIDE REAL LIFE FROM HIM, YOUR MAJESTY, PERHAPS HE SHOULD EXPERIENCE HOW HARD LIFE IS, JUST ONCE, WHO KNOWS...

THE KING LOOKS BACK AGAIN,

A WILTED FLOWER! THE GARDENER RESPONSIBLE FOR THIS IS FIRED,

49

THEY GO BACK TO THE PALACE.

YOU REQUIRE THE IMPOSSIBLE, JUST LET YOUR SON GO AND YOU WILL SEE THAT...

HE'LL DISCOVER FOR HIMSELF HOW GOOD IT IS HERE.

THE KING CAN'T SLEEP...

IT'S NOT A BAD PLAN, IF THAT ASITA HADN'T... I WOULD HAVE AGREED STRAIGHT-AWAY...

HE TELLS HIMSELF THAT HIS SON'S GLOOMINESS IS JUST A PASSING PHASE.

I WAS HARD ON HIM IN THE PAST, PERHAPS IT IS BEST TO WAIT A BIT LONGER.

BUT THE SITUATION ONLY GETS WORSE.

!

I'M NOT HUNGRY.

HE TURNS DOWN FOOD.

WHEN DANCERS TRY TO ATTRACT HIS ATTENTION, HE SHUTS HIS EYES.

HE ONLY LOOKS AT DEAD FLOWERS.

ONE NIGHT WHEN HE CANNOT SLEEP, HE GETS DRESSED AND LEAVES THE BEDCHAMBER.

THE KING ISN'T SLEEPING EITHER.

THE KING IS SUNK IN THOUGHT.

GHARRRRR

?!

I HAVE SUCH A STRANGE FEELING, MY SON. SURELY YOU'RE NOT GOING TO TELL ME THAT YOU...

FATHER, I CAN'T STAND IT HERE ANY LONGER, COULD I GO AWAY FOR A FEW DAYS?

WHO KNOWS WHAT A FEW HARD KNOCKS..?

GO ON THEN, I GIVE UP.

HE DISAPPEARS ON HIS HORSE, KANTAKA.

THE KING SUMMONS...

QUICK, FOLLOW MY SON, DON'T LOSE SIGHT OF HIM!

ARE WE BEING FOLLOWED?

THE PRINCE EXHORTS HIS HORSE TO GO FASTER.

KHATAK KHATAK

LET'S GO BACK, IT'S IMPOSSIBLE TO KEEP UP WITH THAT PAIR.

SO THEY GIVE UP THE CHASE.

FINALLY SIDDHARTHA IS ALONE.

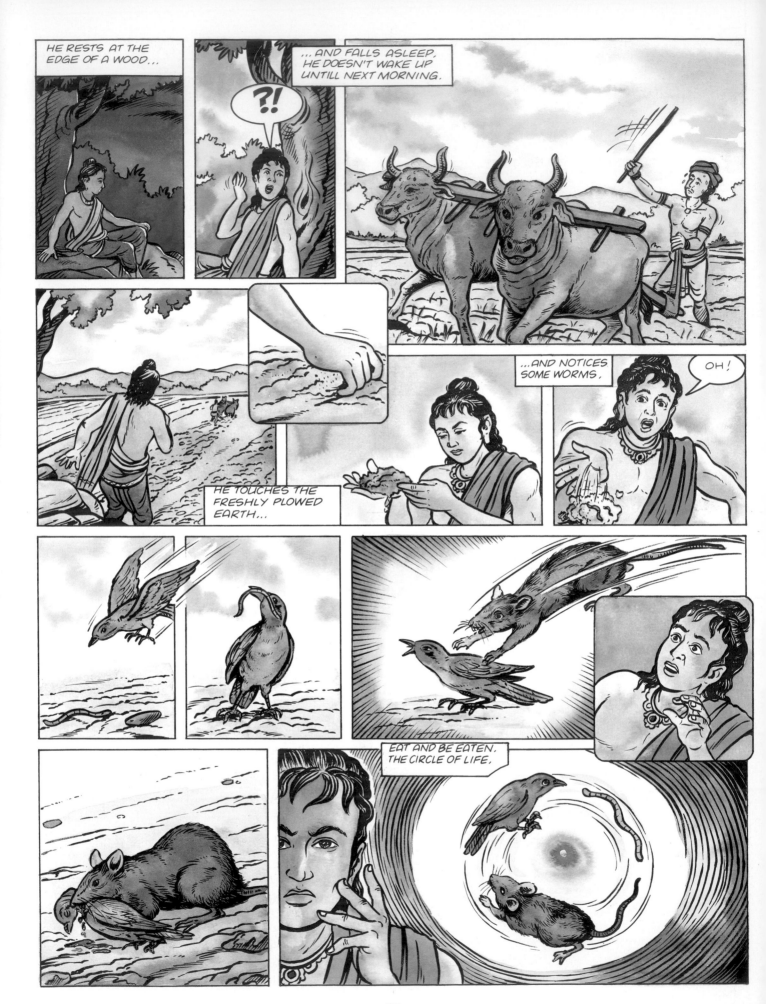

THE PRINCE SINKS FURTHER AWAY IN HIS THOUGHTS.

HE THINKS : THAT PEASANT OVER THERE, IS HE HAPPY?

?

GOD AND THE REDEMPTION OF THE SOUL... DO THESE THINGS EXIST?

SIDDHARTHA IS DYING TO KNOW WHETHER ANYTHING IS INTRANSIENT.

I MUST FIND THE ANSWER TO MY QUESTION, KANTAKA, LET'S RETURN TO THE PALACE.

53

OH MY SON, I'M SO GLAD THAT...

THE KING EMBRACES SIDDHARTHA.

BACK IN THE PALACE, HE FINDS THE KING STILL AWAKE.

I'M SORRY FATHER, BUT I HAVE NOT COME BACK TO STAY FOR EVER.

?

YOU HAVE GIVEN YOUR FATHER SUCH GREAT SORROW.

BELIEVE ME, FATHER, MY SORRY MAY BE EVEN GREATER THAN YOURS. I HAVE TO GO.

BUT THINK OF YOUR TASK, THINK OF THE ROLE ALLOTTED TO YOU.

I CANNOT EXPLAIN, FATHER, BUT I KNOW THAT A MUCH MORE IMPORTANT TASK HAS BEEN ALLOTTED TO ME.

BUT DON'T YOU LOVE ME, YOUR WIFE AND YOUR CHILD?

BUT SIDDHARTHA LEAVES THE PLACE.

THAT IS PRECISELY WHY I WANT TO GO, FATHER. I WANT TO GIVE YOU SOMETHING THAT IS MUCH MORE VALUABLE THAN MATERIAL POSSESSIONS.

WAIT, SIDDHARTHA, WAIT!

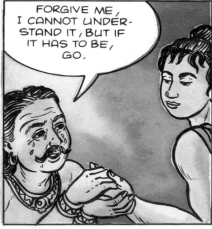

FORGIVE ME, I CANNOT UNDERSTAND IT, BUT IF IT HAS TO BE, GO.

WITHOUT LOOKING AROUND HE WALKS AWAY.

SIDDHARTHA TIPTOES INTO THE ROOM WHERE HIS WIFE AND CHILD ARE SLEEPING.

FAREWELL, DARLING, MAY THINGS GO WELL WITH YOU, MY BOY, IF ONLY YOU KNEW HOW MUCH I LOVE YOU.

SIDDHARTHA STEALS AWAY LIKE A THIEF IN THE NIGHT.

HE LOOKS BACK. A SHADOW IS WAVING FAREWELL.

I'M SORRY FOR ALL OF THEM, KANTAKA, BUT I WILL NOT RETURN UNTILL I HAVE FOUND THE ANSWER TO MY QUESTION.

THE NEXT MORNING HE IS BACK AT THE HILL ON THE SIDE OF THE VALLEY.

HE SEES THE PEASANT IN THE FIELD.

YOU LOOK LIKE YOU COULD USE A HORSE.

WHAT?

IF ONLY I HAD THE MONEY.

IF YOU GIVE ME YOUR CLOTHES, YOU CAN HAVE MY HORSE.

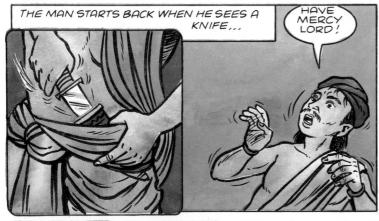

THE MAN STARTS BACK WHEN HE SEES A KNIFE...

HAVE MERCY LORD!

THE PRINCE CUTS OFF HIS HAIR.

THE PEASANT CAN'T BELIEVE HIS EYES.

ARE YOU BEING SERIOUS?

I'M TRULY GRATEFUL. MAY THE GODS BE WITH YOU!

SIDDHARTHA FEELS RELIEVED.

I'M SORRY, KANTAKA, BUT HENCEFORTH OUR PATHS WILL GO SEPERATE WAYS.

TAKE GOOD CARE OF MY HORSE, I WILL CERTAINLY BE BACK ONE DAY.

SIDDHARTHA WALKS DEEPER AND DEEPER INTO THE WOODS.

ANIMALS APPEAR FROM THEIR HIDING PLACE TO SEE HIM.

DUSK FALLS AND MANY OF THE GRADUATES OF THE FOREST GATHER ROUND THE PRINCE.

FOR THE FIRST TIME HE FEELS TRULY ALONE AND YET NOT ALONE.

57

WHO ARE YOU?

THE NEXT MORNING HE FINDS HIMSELF IN THE COMPANY OF FIVE NAKED ASCETICS.

HERMITS OF THE FOREST, TO WHAT DO I OWE THIS VISIT?

I UNDERSTAND THE LANGUAGE OF THE ANIMALS AND I HEARD THAT A GREAT SPIRIT HAD ENTERED OUR FOREST.

MAY I ASK YOU WHERE YOU ARE FROM, MASTER?

SIDDHARTHA IS TAKEN ABACK.

HE LOOKS AT THE HERMIT'S NAIL IN DISGUST.

THE PAST IS UNIMPORTANT, FRIENDS, ONLY THE PRESENT COUNTS.

MAY I ASK YOU SOMETHING? WHY DO YOU NEGLECT YOUR BODY SO?

IS THIS REALLY NECESSARY TO ACHIEVE SELF KNOWLEDGE?

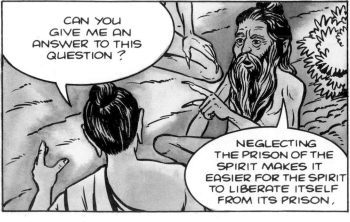

CAN YOU GIVE ME AN ANSWER TO THIS QUESTION?

NEGLECTING THE PRISON OF THE SPIRIT MAKES IT EASIER FOR THE SPIRIT TO LIBERATE ITSELF FROM ITS PRISON.

PERHAPS THESE MEN ARE RIGHT, THE MOST DELICIOUS FOOD AND THE MOST BEAUTIFUL CLOTHES CANNOT MAKE A PERSON HAPPY. I SHALL INVESTIGATE WHETHER THEIR PATH IS THE RIGHT ONE.

YEARS PASS, THE PRISON OF SIDDHARTHA'S MIND GROWS MORE AND MORE FRAGILE, AND HIS HAIR GROWS LONGER AND LONGER.

SOMETIMES IT SEEMS AS THOUGH THE LAST VESTIGES OF LIFE HAVE DEPARTED FROM HIS BODY.

THE LITTLE FOOD HE EATS HE PICKS FROM SHRUBS AND TREES.

SOMETIMES HE SITS MOTIONLESS IN THE RAIN FOR DAYS ON END... OR IN THE BURNING SUN.

THE ANIMALS OF THE FORREST VISIT HIM DAILY.

HAVE YOU EVER MET ANYONE WHO WORKS AT HIS LIBERATION AS STEADFASTLY AS SIDDHARTHA?

EVERY DAY THE FIVE ASCETICS QUIETLY SIT DOWN AT SIDDHARTHA'S FEET,

I AM SURE THAT SIDDHARTHA WILL SOON ACHIEVE THE STATE OF ENLIGHTEN- MENT,

THE ASCETS STAY CLOSE TO HIM AWAITING THE GREAT MOMENT,

ONE MORNING, SIDDHARTHA IS SITTING ON THE RIVER BANK. HE HEARS MUSIC.

?!

SUDDENLY THE STRUMMING STOPS...

YOU HAVE TUNED THE STRING TOO TAUT, MAN, TOO TAUT AND IT WILL BREAK.

WHAT?

YES, AND IF IT'S TOO SLACK THERE'S NO MUSIC...

HE REALISES IT'S A QUESTION OF FINDING A MIDDLE WAY.

NOT SUFFI-CIENTLY TAUT!

TOO TAUT!

I LOOK TERRIBLE, I'VE GONE TOO FAR THE OTHER WAY, TOO TAUT, THAT'S IT, I...

STUMBLING, SIDDHARTHA REACHES THE PLACE WHERE HIS MEDITATING COMPANIONS ARE GATHERED.

THEIR BEHAVIOUR IS MUCH TOO EXTREME. THIS IS NOT MY WAY.

THAT'S REFRESHING, SURELY THERE MUST BE A MIDDLE WAY.

DETERMINEDLY SIDDHARTHA RETURNS TO THE RIVER BANK AND HAS A WASH,

HIS WHOLE BODY HURTS, EVERY MOVEMENT IS DIFFICULT,

WHAT IS THE REASON THAT YOU HAVE COME?

I HAVE HAD A CHILD AND I WISH TO MAKE AN OFFER TO NATURE, I THOUGHT THAT YOU WERE THE KING OF THE TREE SPIRITS,

HOW CAN A PERSON NEGLECT HIMSELF SO?

SIDDHARTHA WAKES UP FROM HIS REVERIE,

HESITANTLY, HE STARTS TO EAT,

COULD I USE YOUR KNIFE FOR A MOMENT?

AND SIDDHARTHA CUTS OFF HIS HAIR AND BEARD,

61

THE WOMEN IS ASTONISHED BY HIS NOBLE FEATURES,

FORGIVE ME FOR TAKING YOU FOR A TREE SPIRIT,

HE ASKS HER TO SIT UP,

I AM THE ONE WHO WAS MISTAKEN, I HAVE TUNED MY SPIRIT SO THAT IT WAS MUCH TOO TAUT,

I WENT FROM ONE EXTREME TO THE OTHER,

THANK YOU FOR YOUR KIND CONCERN. I FEEL REBORN,

THE HERMITS HAVE SEEN EVERYTHING,

MASTER, YOU HAVE BROKEN YOUR VOW,

WE SAW YOU TALKING TO A WOMAN,

THAT'S TRUE, BUT HENCEFORTH I DON'T CARE ABOUT VOWS ANY MORE,

NEITHER A LIFE OF PLEASURE NOR A LIFE OF SELF-CHASTISEMENT LEADS TO INSIGHT,

I THINK HE HAS LOST THE PATH,

COME, LET US GO,

SIDDHARTHA THINKS : LIFE IS MOVEMENT, BUT THESE MAN ARE RIGID,

THE BANKS COME TOGETHER SOMEWHERE BETWEEN THIS SIDE AND THE OTHER SIDE. I MUST FOLLOW THE MIDDLE PATH,

AFTER A LONG SEARCH SIDDHARTHA FINDS A SUITABLE TREE TO MEDITATE UNDER.

COULD I BE SO FREE AS TO TAKE SOME GRASS?

TAKE AS MUCH AS YOU LIKE, LORD.

HE GATHERS THE GRASS TO MAKE A BED OF STRAW.

THIS GRASS IS BEAUTIFULLY SOFT, WHY SHOULD A PERSON TORTURE HIS BODY SO?

I WILL NOT LEAVE THIS PLACE UNTIL I HAVE DISCOVERED THE DEEPER MEANING OF LIFE.

WHO IS THIS?

SIDDHARTHA'S DETERMINATION IS NOTICED EVEN IN HELL.

I, MARA, THE GOD OF HELL, WILL QUICKLY HAVE TO PUT A STOP TO THIS.

MARA SUMMONS HIS DAUGHTERS TO HIM.

MY DAUGHTERS, YOU KNOW THAT MAN-KIND MUST REMAIN IN IGNORANCE. QUICKLY, TEMPT AND MISLEAD HIM!

EVERY MAN IS MOVED BY GOD'S MOST BEAUTIFUL CREATIONS,

AFTER ALL, SIDDHARTHA IS ONLY A MAN,

AND SURELY HE WILL BE TEMPTED...

...BY THE PLEASURES OF THE FLESH...

...AND A WARM, SOFT EMBRACE.

BUT MARA'S PLAN FAILS.

STUPID WOMEN, I THINK I WILL HAVE TO DO IT MYSELF.

MARA SETS HORDES OF TERRIFYING DEMONS ON SIDDHARTHA.

NOTHING APPEARS TO INTERRUPT HIS MEDITATION.

THEN MARA TRIES TO SOFTEN SIDDHARTHA'S HEART BY CONJURING UP THE PRINCE'S PAST.

WHY SHOULD YOU FIND WHAT SO MANY HAVE SOUGHT IN VAIN? GO BACK HOME. THE KING NEEDS YOU. SO DOES YOUR WIFE AND YOUR SON. DON'T WASTE YOUR TIME ANY LONGER.

FINALLY HE ASSUMES THE FORM OF THE PRINCE HIMSELF.

EVERYONE WILL BE CONVINCED THAT YOU ARE A GREAT RULER, BUT NO ONE WILL WITNESS YOUR ENLIGHTENMENT.

LISTEN TO THESE WORDS AND RETURN TO THE PALACE.

THE EARTH HERE BELOW MY HAND WILL BE MY WITNESS.

THEN MARA REALIZES THAT HE HAS BEEN DEFEATED AND DISAPPEARS FROM THE PRINCE'S MIND.

AMIDST ALL THIS TRANSIENCE, IS THERE ANYTHING WHICH IS NOT SUBJECT TO CHANGE?

BIRTH IS THE CAUSE OF OLD AGE AND SICKNESS,

BIRTH IS THE RESULT OF DESIRE FOR FOOD AND SENSUAL DELIGHT,

DESIRE LEADS TO THE QUEST FOR PLEASURE, GREED AND AN ATTACHMENT TO MATERIAL POSSESSIONS,

IS IT NOT POSSIBLE TO BREAK THIS CHAIN IN WHICH MAN IS IMPRISONED AND IN WHICH MEN IMPRISON EACH OTHER? CAN'T A PERSON BREAK AWAY FROM THIS WHEEL OF REBIRTH?

IT IS ONLY BY NOT IDENTIFYING WITH THE SENSES, THE SPOKES OF THE WHEEL, THAT MAN CAN FREE HIMSELF FROM ILLUSIONS,

THE OBSERVER IS THE CENTRE OF THE WHEEL, ALWAYS DETACHED FROM EVERYTHING,

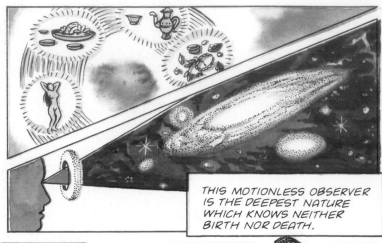

THIS MOTIONLESS OBSERVER IS THE DEEPEST NATURE WHICH KNOWS NEITHER BIRTH NOR DEATH,

FOR MANY DAYS HE REMAINS SEATED IN SUPREME PEACE,

LIKE THAT LITTLE BIRD I MAY NOT KEEP MY SONG TO MYSELF EITHER,

AND THUS PRINCE SIDDHARTHA CHANGED INTO SIDDHARTHA THE BUDDHA AND ENTERED THE WORLD 2500 YEARS AGO, SO THAT EVERYONE COULD SHARE HIS EXPERIENCE OF LASTING PEACE AND HAPPINESS,
MAY ALL LIVING CREATURES FIND THE SAME JOY AND PEACE WITHIN THEMSELVES.

THE END